Selected Poems

by the same author

New Territory
The War Horse
In Her Own Image
Night Feed
The Journey

EAVAN BOLAND
Selected Poems

CARCANET

First published in 1989 by
Carcanet Press Limited
208-212 Corn Exchange Buildings
Manchester M4 3BQ

Published in association with WEB
c/o Argus Press, 12 Malpas Street, Dublin 8

British Library Cataloguing in Publication Data
Boland, Eavan, *1944-*
Selected poems.
I. Title
821'.914

ISBN 0-85635-741-3

The Publisher acknowledges financial assistance from
the Arts Council of Great Britain.

Typeset in 10pt Palatino by Bryan Williamson, Manchester
Printed in England by SRP Ltd, Exeter

*For Kevin, Sarah
and Eavan Frances*

Contents

from *New Territory*

from *The War Horse*

from *In Her Own Image*

from *Night Feed*

from *The Journey*

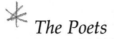

The Poets

They, like all creatures, being made
For the shovel and worm,
Ransacked their perishable minds and found
Pattern and form
And with their own hands quarried from hard words
A figure in which secret things confide.

They are abroad: their spirits like a pride
Of lions circulate,
Are desperate, just as the jewelled beast,
That lion constellate,
Whose scenery is Betelgeuse and Mars,
Hunts without respite among fixed stars.

And they prevail: to his undoing every day
The essential sun
Proceeds, but only to accommodate
A tenant moon,
And he remains until the very break
Of morning, absentee landlord of the dark.

The Pilgrim

FOR EAMON GRENNAN

When the nest falls in winter, birds have flown
To distant lights and hospitality.
The pilgrim, with his childhood home a ruin,
Shares their fate and, like them, suddenly
Becomes a tenant of the wintry day.
Looking back, out of the nest of stone
As it tumbles, he can see his childhood
Flying away like an evicted bird.

Underground although the ground is bare,
Summer is turning on her lights. Spruce
And larch and massive chestnut will appear
Above his head in leaf. Oedipus
Himself, cold and sightless, was aware
Of no more strife or drama at Colonus:
He became, when he could go no further,
Just an old man hoping for warm weather.

At journey's end in the waters of a shrine,
No greater thing will meet him than the shock
Of his own human face, beheaded in
The holy pool. Steadily he must look
At this unshriven thing among the bells
And offerings, and for his penance mark
How his aspiring days like fallen angels
Follow one another into the dark.

New Territory

Several things announced the fact to us:
The captain's Spanish tears
Falling like doubloons in the headstrong light,
And then of course the fuss –
The crew jostling and interspersing cheers
With wagers. Overnight
As we went down to our cabins, nursing the last
Of the grog, talking as usual of conquest,
Land hove into sight.

Frail compasses and trenchant constellations
Brought us as far as this,
And now air and water, fire and earth
Stand at their given stations
Out there, and are ready to replace
This single desperate width
Of ocean. Why do we hesitate? Water and air
And fire and earth and therefore life are here,
And therefore death.

10

Out of the dark man comes to life and into it
He goes and loves and dies,
(His element being the dark and not the light of day)
So the ambitious wit
Of poets and exploring ships have been his eyes –
Riding the dark for joy –
And so Isaiah of the sacred text is eagle-eyed because
By peering down the unlit centuries
He glimpsed the holy boy.

Mirages

At various times strenuous sailing men
Claim to have seen creatures of myth
Scattering light at the furthest points of dawn –

Creatures too seldom seen to reward the patience
Of a night-watch, who provide no ready encore
But like the stars revisit generations.

And kings riding to battle on the advice
Of their ambition have seen crosses burn
In the skylight of the winter solstice.

Reasonable men, however hold aloof,
Doubting the gesture, speech and anecdote
Of those who touch the Grail and bring no proof –

Failing to recognise that in their fast
Ethereal way, mirages are
This daylight world in summary and forecast.

So a prince, a fledgling still and far
From coronation, kept at home,
Will draw his sword and murder empty air –

And should his father die and that death bring
Him majesty, his games have been his school,
His phantom war a forcing house of kings.

11

Migration

From August they embark on every wind,
Managing with grace
This new necessity, widely determined
On a landing place.
Daredevil swallows, coloured swifts go forth
Like some great festival removing south.

Cuckoo and operatic nightingale
Meeting like trains of thought
Concluding summer, in complete agreement, file
Towards the sea at night,
And find at last their bright geometry
(Triumphant overland) is not seaworthy.

Sandpiper, finch and wren and goldencrest,
Whose baffled
Movements start or finish summer, now at last
Return, single and ruffled,
And lift up their voices in a world of light,
And choose their loves as though determined to forget.

As though upon their travels, as each bird
Fell down to die, the sea
Had opened, showing those above a graveyard
Without sanctity –
Birds and their masters, many beautiful,
Tumbled together without name or burial.

Lullaby

FROM A NARRATIVE POEM

O nurse, when I was a rascal boy, bold
February winds were snaffling gold
Out of the crocuses; there in grief
For the pretty, gaudy things I'd cry: "Stop thief"
And you would grumble: "Child, let be, let be."

Or we would come across a sapling tree
To discover frost sipping its new blood;
I'd join my arms around its perished wood
And weep, and you would say: "Now child, its place
Is in a merry heart, not your embrace."
And one April morning that was filled
With mating tunes, a nest of finches spilled
Which slipped its flowering anchor in a gale.
I cupped one in my fingers, dead and small.
But late that night you stole to me on tiptoe
and whispered: "Child, child, the winds must blow."

Requiem for a Personal Friend
ON A HALF-EATEN BLACKBIRD

A striped philistine with quick
Sight, quiet paws, today –
In gorging on a feathered prey –
Filleted our garden's music.

Such robbery in such a mouthful!
Here rests, shovelled under simple
Vegetables, my good example –
Singing daily, daily faithful.

No conceit and not contrary –
My best colleague, worst of all,
Was half-digested, his sweet whistle
Swallowed like a dictionary.

Little victim, song for song –
Who share a trade must share a threat –
So I write to cheat the cat
Who got your body, of my tongue.

From the Painting 'Back from Market' by Chardin

Dressed in the colours of a country day –
Grey-blue, blue-grey, the white of seagull's bodies –
Chardin's peasant woman
Is to be found at all times in her short delay
Of dreams, her eyes mixed
Between love and market, empty flagons of wine
At her feet, bread under her arm. He has fixed
Her limbs in colour, and her heart in line.

In her right hand, the hindlegs of a hare
Peep from a cloth sack; through the door
Another woman moves
In painted daylight; nothing in this bare
Closet has been lost
Or changed. I think of what great art removes:
Hazard and death, the future and the past,
This woman's secret history and her loves –

And even the dawn market, from whose bargaining
She has just come back, where men and women
Congregate and go
Among the produce, learning to live from morning
To next day, linked
By a common impulse to survive, although
In surging light they are single and distinct,
Like birds in the accumulating snow.

The Flight of the Earls
FOR BRENDAN KENNELLY

Princes it seems are seldom wise:
Most of them fall for a woman's tears
Or else her laughter, such as Paris
Whose decision stretched to ten alarming years –
Nothing would suit
Until he'd brought
The kingdom down around his ears.

Now in the middle ages see
The legendary boy of king and queen:
A peacock of all chivalry,
He dies at twenty on some battle-green
And ever since
The good Black Prince
Rides to the land of might-have-been.

Whether our own were foolish or wise
Hardly concerns us; death ran away with our chances
Of a meeting, yet we strain our eyes
Hoping perhaps just one with his golden flounces
Has outwitted theft.
So are we left
Writing to headstones and forgotten princes.

After the Irish of Egan O'Rahilly

Without flocks or cattle or the curved horns
Of cattle, in a drenching night without sleep,
My five wits on the famous uproar
Of the wave toss like ships,
And I cry for boyhood, long before
Winkle and dogfish had defiled my lips.

O if he lived, the prince who sheltered me,
And his company who gave me entry
On the river of the Laune,
Whose royalty stood sentry
Over intricate harbours, I and my own
Would not be desolate in Dermot's country.

Fierce McCarthy Mor whose friends were welcome.
McCarthy of the Lee, a slave of late,
McCarthy of Kanturk whose blood
Has dried underfoot:
Of all my princes not a single word –
Irrevocable silence ails my heart,

15

My heart shrinks in me, my heart ails
That every hawk and royal hawk is lost;
From Cashel to the far sea
Their birthright is dispersed
Far and near, night and day, by robbery
And ransack, every town oppressed.

Take warning wave, take warning crown of the sea,
I, O'Rahilly – witless from your discords –
Were Spanish sails again afloat
And rescue on your tides,
Would force this outcry down your wild throat,
Would make you swallow these Atlantic words.

Athene's Song

FOR MY FATHER

From my father's head I sprung
Goddess of the war, created
Partisan and soldiers' physic –
My symbols boast and brazen gong –
Until I made in Athens wood
Upon my knees a new music.

When I played my pipe of bone,
Robbed and whittled from a stag,
Every bird became a lover
Every lover to its tone
Found the truth of song and brag;
Fish sprung in the full river.

Peace became the toy of power
When other noises broke my sleep:
Like dreams I saw the hot ranks
And heroes in another flower
Than any there; I dropped my pipe
Remembering their shouts, their thanks.

16

Beside the water, lost and mute,
Lies my pipe and like my mind
Remains unknown, remains unknown
And in some hollow taking part
With my heart against my hand,
Holds its peace and holds its own.

The War Horse

This dry night, nothing unusual
About the clip, clop, casual

Iron of his shoes as he stamps death
Like a mint on the innocent coinage of earth.

I lift the window, watch the ambling feather
Of hock and fetlock, loosed from its daily tether

In the tinker camp on the Enniskerry Road,
Pass, his breath hissing, his snuffling head

Down. He is gone. No great harm is done.
Only a leaf of our laurel hedge is torn –

Of distant interest like a maimed limb,
Only a rose which now will never climb

The stone of our house, expendable, a mere
Line of defence against him, a volunteer

You might say, only a crocus its bulbous head
Blown from growth, one of the screamless dead.

But we, we are safe, our unformed fear
Of fierce commitment gone; why should we care

If a rose, a hedge, a crocus are uprooted
Like corpses, remote, crushed, mutilated?

He stumbles on like a rumour of war, huge,
Threatening; neighbours use the subterfuge

Of curtains; he stumbles down our short street
Thankfully passing us. I pause, wait,

Then to breathe relief lean on the sill
And for a second only my blood is still

With atavism. That rose he smashed frays
Ribboned across our hedge, recalling days

Of burned countryside, illicit braid:
A cause ruined before, a world betrayed.

Child of Our Time

FOR AENGUS

Yesterday I knew no lullaby
But you have taught me overnight to order
This song, which takes from your final cry
Its tune, from your unreasoned end its reason;
Its rhythm from the discord of your murder,
Its motive from the fact you cannot listen.

We who should have known how to instruct
With rhymes for your waking, rhythms for your sleep
Names for the animals you took to bed,
Tales to distract, legends to protect,
Later an idiom for you to keep
And living, learn, must learn from you, dead –

To make our broken images rebuild
Themselves around your limbs, your broken
Image, find for your sake whose life our idle
Talk has cost, a new language. Child
Of our time, our times have robbed your cradle.
Sleep in a world your final sleep has woken.

The Famine Road

"Idle as trout in light Colonel Jones
these Irish, give them no coins at all; their bones
need toil, their characters no less." Trevelyan's
seal blooded the deal table. The Relief
Committee deliberated: "Might it be safe,
Colonel, to give them roads, roads to force
from nowhere, going nowhere of course?"

> *"One out of every ten and then*
> *another third of those again*
> *women – in a case like yours."*

Sick, directionless they worked; fork, stick
were iron years away; after all could
they not blood their knuckles on rock, suck
April hailstones for water and for food?
Why for that, cunning as housewives, each eyed –
as if at a corner butcher – the other's buttock.

> *"Anything may have caused it, spores,*
> *a childhood accident; one sees*
> *day after day these mysteries."*

Dusk: they will work tomorrow without him.
They know it and walk clear; he has become
a typhoid pariah, his blood tainted, although
he shares it with some there. No more than snow
attends its own flakes where they settle
and melt, will they pray by his death rattle.

> *"You never will, never you know*
> *but take it well woman, grow*
> *your garden, keep house, goodbye."*

"It has gone better than we expected, Lord
Trevelyan, sedition, idleness, cured
in one; from parish to parish, field to field,
the wretches work till they are quite worn,

then fester by their work; we march the corn
to the ships in peace; this Tuesday I saw bones
out of my carriage window, your servant Jones."

"Barren, never to know the load
of his child in you, what is your body
now if not a famine road?"

Cyclist with Cut Branches

Country hands on the handlebars,
A bicycle bisecting cars
  Lethal and casual
In rush hour traffic, I remember
Seeing, as I watched that September
  For you as usual.

Like rapid mercury abused
By summer heat where it is housed
  In slender telling glass,
My heart taking grief's temperature,
That summer, lost its power to cure,
  It's gift to analyse

Jasmine and the hyacinth,
The lintel mortar and the plinth
  Of spring across his bars,
Like globed grapes at first I thought,
Then at last more surely wrought
  Like winter's single stars.

Until I glimpsed not him but you
Like an animal the packs pursue
  To covert in a forest,
And knew the branches were not spring's
Nor ever summer's ample things,
  But decay's simple trust,

And since we had been like them cut
But from the flowering not the root
   Then we had thanks to give –
That they and we had opened once,
Had found the light, had lost its glance
   And still had lives to live.

Song

Where in blind files
Bats outsleep the frost
Water slips through stones
Too fast, too fast
For ice; afraid he'd slip
By me I asked him first.

Round as a bracelet
Clasping the wet grass,
An adder drowsed by berries
Which change blood to cess;
Dreading delay's venom
I risked the first kiss.

My skirt in my hand,
Lifting the hem high
I forded the river there;
Drops splashed my thigh.
Ahead of me at last
He turned at my cry:

"Look how the water comes
Boldly to my side;
See the waves attempt
What you have never tried."
He late that night
Followed the leaping tide.

The Botanic Gardens

FOR KEVIN

Guided by love, leaving aside dispute –
Guns on the pages of newspapers, the sound
Urgent of peace – we drive in real pursuit
Of another season, spring, where each has found
Something before, new, and then sense
In the Botanic Gardens, terms of reference.

You take my hand. Three years ago, your bride,
I felt your heart in darkness, a full moon
Hauling mine to it like a tide.
Still at night our selves reach to join.
To twine like these trees in peace and stress
Before the peril of unconsciousness.

Corsican pine, guerilla poison plants –
The first gardener here by foreign carriage
And careful seeding in this circumference
Imitated the hours of our marriage:
The flowers of forced proximity, swollen, fed,
Flourishing here, usually sheltered,

Exposed this once. Now you have overstepped
My reach, searching for something this February
Like a scholar in poor light over a script,
Able at last to decipher its coded story
And so preoccupied you do not see
My absence in the conservatory

Where you, while African grotesqueries
Sweat in sandy heat, at last stand
Wondering at cacti, deformed trees
Most ridicule. Each pumpkin history
Turns coach at a touch of your hand.
I watch and love you in your mystery.

Prisoners

I saw him first lost in the lion cages
Of the zoo; before he could tear it out
I screamed my heart out; but his rages
Had been left behind. All he had left was his lope,
his mane, as – bored as a socialite
With her morning post – I saw him slit
A rabbit open like an envelope.

Everything after that was parody –
I glimpsed him at the hearth in a jet
Cat, in a school annual tamed in type,
In a screen safari. The irony
Of finding him here in the one habitat
I never expected, alive and well in our suburban
World, present as I garden, sweep,

Wring the teacloth dry, domesticate
Acanthus in a bowl, orbit each chair
Exactly round our table. Your pullover
Lies on the bed upstairs, spread there where
You can no more free yourself from the bars
Of your arms round me than can over
Us the lion flee, silently, his stars.

Ready for Flight

From this I will not swerve nor fall nor falter:
If around your heart the crowds disperse,
And I who at their whim now freeze or swelter
Am allowed to come to a more temperate place,

And if a runner starts to run to me
Dispatched by you, crying that all is trampled
Underfoot, terraces smashed, the entry
Into holy places rudely sampled,

Then I would come at once my love with love
Bringing to wasted areas the sight
Of butterfly and swan and turtle dove
Their wings ruffled like sails ready for flight

In such surroundings, after the decease
Of devils, you and I would live in peace.

Sisters

FOR NESSA, MY OWN

Now it is winter and the hare
Imitates the hillside snow,
Crouches in his frame of ice,
The dormouse in his wheel of fur,
While in caves hour by hour
The bat glistens in reverse.

Snowdrops poised for assassination
Broadcast, white in the face, the stress
Of first bursting out of a prison
Where winter grips the warder's keys
By day, then at the dusk's tilt
Loops them to Orion's belt.

In Monkstown bay a young seal
Surfaces, sleuth hound of herring;
Gulls shriek as he steals their meal
But I, getting the hint of spring
As a fisherman an Armada hull,
Welcome his unexpected skull.

For you, as his outline through
The Spring tide comes to view,
Spring to mind. In such disguise
Our love survived, as the sea with ease
Becomes with granite a graphic twin
Tumbling like a harlequin.

24

At seven years, the age of reason,
The ready child communicates
With Christ, according to our church.
Seven years ago in the silly season
And for such reasons our two hearts
Were put outside each other's reach.

The fable goes: becoming warmer
Every second against his breast,
Christ's blood created the first informer,
The robin redbreast: and still the thirst
For knowledge and blood, they still remain,
And still we turn to still the pain.

For it was I, I who betrayed
By letters unwritten, unlifted 'phones,
Unspoken words and now would have
You and those seven years re-made,
That I exhume these sad bones,
I who wish them another grave.

No shoulders, not a "soldier on",
No gunshots, nothing of that kind:
We both knew soldiers are unknown.
But since you hauled my one eye blind,
Round like the morning globe to meet
Light, could my thanks be discreet?

O and my sister, not a sound
Could bribe its way into this silence,
Nor ricochet where you have found
In one stunned heart, which must now trounce
Breaking, if not a breathing space,
Well then a sister's grim embrace.

And in your ear a final word
That we remember all our pain
Has saved us from a final fate,
One worse than death, has left us scarred
But strangely safe for we remain
From these others separate:

The three harridans who toy
With human life, who in the cut
And thrust of gossip, never
Noticed one untwisted joy,
One sisterhood, so could not sever
Ours with an idle, chill gesture

Elegy for a Youth Changed to a Swan
FROM LIR, THE IRISH LEGEND

Now the March woods will miss his step,
Finding out a way at spring's start
To break at once their bracken and their sleep,
And now have lost, robbed of their rightful part,
Some hawk a master's hand, some maid a heart.

Urchins of the hurdled hawthorn, sparrows,
Spiders webbed in hedges, brown
Field mice, wheeled, sleeping in their furrows,
Spared by the plough and stout with corn –
These were familiars of Lir's son

No less than the stiff, aloof lily,
The oak and the hawk, the Moy salmon
On February mornings, unruly
With new life, and the flushed rowan
Stooped with berries, October's paragon.

O sap of the green forest like a sea
Rise in the sycamore and rowan,
Rise in the wild plum and chestnut tree
Until the woods become a broad ocean
For my son in his wilderness, my swan,

That he may see breaking on his breast
And wings not the waters of his exile,
Nor the pawn of the wind, the cold crest,
But branches of the white beam and the maple,
Boughs of the almond and the laurel.

O Fons Bandusiae

HORACE 3: XIII

Bold as crystal, bright as glass,
Your waters leap while we appear
Carrying to your woodland shrine
Gifts below your worthiness:
Grape and flower, Bandusia,
Yellow hawksbeard, ready wine.

And tomorrow we will bring
A struggling kid, his temples sore
With early horns, as sacrifice.
Tomorrow his new trumpeting
Will come to nothing, when his gore
Stains and thaws your bright ice.

Canicula, the lamp of drought,
The summer's fire, leaves your grace
Inviolate in the woods where
Every day you spring to comfort
The broad bull in his trace,
The herd out of the shepherd's care:

With every fountain, every spring
Of legend, I will set you down
In praise and immortal spate:
These waters which drop gossiping
To ground, this wet surrounding stone
And this green oak I celebrate.

Suburban Woman

I

Town and country at each other's throat –
between a space of truce until one night

walls began to multiply, to spawn
like lewd whispers of the goings-on,

27

the romperings, the rape on either side,
the smiling killing, that you were better dead

than let them get you. But they came, armed
with blades and ladders, with slimed

knives, day after day, week by week –
a proxy violation. She woke

one morning to the usual story: withdrawing,
neither side had gained, but there, dying,

caught in cross-fire, her past lay, bleeding
from wounds each meant for each, which needing

each other for other wars they could not inflict
one on another. Haemorrhaging to hacked

roads, to where in back gardens, like a pride
of lions toiled for booty, tribal acres died

and her world with them. She saw their power to sever
with a scar. She is the sole survivor.

II

Morning: mistress of talcums, spun
and second cottons, run tights
she is, courtesan to the lethal
rapine of routine. The room invites.
She reaches to fluoresce the dawn.
The kitchen lights like a brothel.

III

The chairs dusted and the morning
coffee break behind, she starts pawning

her day again to the curtains, the red
carpets, the stair rods, at last to the bed,

28

the unmade bed where once in an underworld
of limbs, her eyes freckling the night like jewelled

lights on a cave wall, she, crying, stilled,
bargained out of nothingness her child,

bartered from the dark her only daughter.
Waking, her cheeks dried, to a brighter

dawn she sensed in her as in April earth
a seed, a life ransoming her death.

IV

Late, quiet across her garden
sunlight shifts like a cat
burglar, thieving perspectives,
leaving her in the last light
alone, where, as shadows harden,
lengthen, silent she perceives
veteran dead-nettles, knapweed
crutched on walls, a summer's seed
of roses trenched in ramsons, and stares
at her life falling with her flowers,
like military tribute or the tears
of shell-shocked men, into arrears.

V

Her kitchen blind down – a white flag –
the day's assault over, now she will shrug

a hundred small surrenders off as images
still born, unwritten metaphors, blank pages;

and on this territory, blindfold, we meet
at last, veterans of a defeat

no truce will heal, no formula prevent
breaking out fresh again; again the print

of twigs stalking her pillow will begin
a new day and all her victims then –

hopes unreprieved, hours taken hostage –
will newly wake, while I, on a new page

will watch, like town and country, word, thought
look for ascendancy, poise, retreat,

leaving each line maimed, my forces used.
Defeated we survive, we two, housed

together in my compromise, my craft –
who are of one another the first draft.

Ode to Suburbia

Six o'clock: the kitchen bulbs which blister
Your dark, your housewives starting to nose
Out each other's day, the claustrophobia
Of your back gardens varicose
With shrubs, make an ugly sister
Of you suburbia.

How long ago did the glass in your windows subtly
Silver into mirrors which again
And again show the same woman
Shriek at a child, which multiply
A dish, a brush, ash,
The gape of a fish

In the kitchen, the gape of a child in the cot?
You swelled so that when you tried
The silver slipper on your foot,
It pinched your instep and the common
Hurt which touched you made
You human.

No creatures of your streets will feel the touch
Of a wand turning the wet sinews
Of fruit suddenly to a coach,
While this rat without leather reins
Or a whip or britches continues
Sliming your drains.

No magic here. Yet you encroach until
The shy countryside, fooled
By your plainness falls, then rises
From your bed changed, schooled
Forever by your skill,
Your compromises.

Tirade for the Mimic Muse

I've caught you out. You slut. You fat trout.
So here you are fumed in candle-stink.
Its yellow balm exhumes you for the glass.
How you arch and pout in it!
How you poach your face in it!
Anyone would think you were a whore –
An ageing out-of-work kind-hearted tart.
I know you for the ruthless bitch you are:
Our criminal, our tricoteuse, our Muse –
Our Muse of Mimic Art.

Eye-shadow, swivel brushes, blushers,
Hot pinks, rouge pots, sticks,
Ice for the pores, a mud mask –
All the latest tricks.
Not one of them disguise
That there's a dead millennium in your eyes.
You try to lamp the sockets of your loss:
The lives that famished for your look of love.
Your time is up. There's not a stroke, a flick
Can make your crime cosmetic.

With what drums and dances, what deceits,
Rituals and flatteries of war,
Chants and pipes and witless empty rites
And war-like men
And wet-eyed patient women
You did protect yourself from horrors,
From the lizarding of eyelids
From the whiskering of nipples,
From the slow betrayals of our bedroom mirrors –
How you fled

The kitchen screw and the rack of labour,
The wash thumbed and the dish cracked,
The scream of beaten women,
The crime of babies battered,
The hubbub and the shriek of daily grief
That seeks asylum behind suburb walls –
A world you could have sheltered in your skirts –
And well I know and how I see it now,
The way you latched your belt and itched your hem
And shook it off like dirt.

And I who mazed my way to womanhood
Through all your halls of mirrors, making faces,
To think I waited on your trashy whim!
Hoping your lamp and flash,
Your glass, might show
This world I needed nothing else to know
But love and again love and again love.
In a nappy stink, by a soaking wash
Among stacked dishes
Your glass cracked, your nerve broke,

Your luck ran out. Look. My words leap
Among your pinks, your stench pots and sticks.
They scatter shadow, swivel brushes, blushers.
Make your face naked,
Strip your mind naked,
Drench your skin in a woman's tears.
I will wake you from your sluttish sleep.
I will show you true reflections, terrors.
You are the Muse of all our mirrors.
Look in them and weep.

In Her Own Image

It is her eyes:
the irises are gold
and round they go
like the ring on my wedding finger,
round and round

and I can't touch
their histories or tears.
To think they were once my satellites!
They shut me out now.
Such light years!

She is not myself
anymore, she is not
even in my sky
anymore and I
am not myself.

I will not disfigure
Her pretty face.
Let her wear amethyst thumbprints,
a family heirloom,
a sort of burial necklace

and I know just the place:
Where the wall glooms,
where the lettuce seeds,
where the jasmine springs
no surprises

I will bed her.
She will bloom there,
second nature to me,
the one perfection
among compromises.

In His Own Image

I was not myself, myself.
The celery feathers,
the bacon flitch,
the cups deep on the shelf
and my cheek
coppered and shone
in the kettle's paunch,
my mouth
blubbed in the tin of the pan –
they were all I had to go on.

How could I go on
with such meagre proofs of myself?
I woke day after day.
Day after day I was gone
from the self I was last night.

And then he came home tight.

Such a simple definition!
How did I miss it?
Now I see
that all I needed
was a hand
to mould my mouth,
to scald my cheek,
was this concussion
by whose lights I find
my self-possession,
where I grow complete.

He splits my lip with his fist,
shadows my eye with a blow,
knuckles my neck to its proper angle.
What a perfectionist!

His are a sculptor's hands:
they summon
form from the void,
they bring
me to myself again.
I am a new woman.

Anorexic

Flesh is heretic.
My body is a witch.
I am burning it.

Yes I am torching
her curves and paps and wiles.
They scorch in my self denials.

How she meshed my head
in the half-truths
of her fevers

till I renounced
milk and honey
and the taste of lunch.

I vomited
her hungers.
Now the bitch is burning.

I am starved and curveless.
I am skin and bone.
She has learned her lesson.

Thin as a rib
I turn in sleep.
My dreams probe

a claustrophobia
a sensuous enclosure.
How warm it was and wide

once by a warm drum,
once by the song of his breath
and in his sleeping side.

Only a little more,
only a few more days
sinless, foodless,

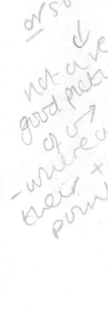

35

I will slip
back into him again
as if I had never been away.

Caged so
I will grow
angular and holy

past pain,
keeping his heart
such company

as will make me forget
in a small space
the fall

into forked dark,
into python needs
heaving to hips and breasts
and lips and heat
and sweat and fat and greed.

Mastectomy

My ears heard
their words.
I didn't believe them.

No, even through my tears
they couldn't deceive me.
Even so

I could see
through them
to the years

opening
their arteries,
fields gulching

into trenches,
cuirasses stenching,
a mulch of heads

and towns
as prone
to bladed men

as women.
How well
I recognized

the specialist
freshing death
across his desk,

the surgeon,
blade-handed,
standing there

urging patience.
How well
they have succeeded!

I have stopped bleeding.
I look down.
It has gone.

So they have taken off
what slaked them first,
what they have hated since:

blue-veined
white-domed
home

of wonder
and the wetness
of their dreams.

I flatten
to their looting,
to the sleight

of their plunder.
I am a brute site.
Theirs is the true booty.

Solitary

Night:
An oratory of dark,
a chapel of unreason.

Here in the shubbery
the shrine.
I am its votary,
its season.

Flames
single
to my fingers

expert
to pick out
their heart,
the sacred heat

none may violate.
You could die for this.
The gods could make you blind.

I defy them.
I know,
only I know

these incendiary
and frenzied ways:
I am alone.

No one's here,
no one sees
my hands

fan and cup,
my thumbs tinder.
How it leaps

from spark to blaze!
I flush
I darken.

How my flesh summers,
how my mind shadows
meshed in this brightness,

how my cry
blasphemes
light and dark,
screams
land from sea,
makes word flesh
that now makes me

animal,
inanimate,
satiate,

and back I go
to a slack tip,
a light.

I stint my worship,
the cold watch I keep.
Fires flint somewhere else.
I winter
into sleep.

Menses

It is dark again.

I am sick of it,
filled with it,
dulled by it,
thick with it.

To be the mere pollution of her wake!
a water cauled by her light,
a slick haul,
a fallen self,
a violence,
a daughter.

I am the moon's looking glass.
My days are moon-dials.
She will never be done with me.
She needs me.
She is dry.

I leash to her,
a sea,
a washy heave,
a tide.
Only my mind is free

among the ruffian growths,
the bindweed
and the meadowsweet,
the riff-raff of my garden.

How I envy them:
each filament,
each anther bred
from its own style,
its stamen,
is to itself a christening,
is to itself a marriage bed.

40

They fall to earth,
so ignorant,
so innocent,
of the sweated waters
and the watered salts,
of ecstasy,
of birth.

They are street-walkers,
lesbians,
nuns.
I am not one of them –

and how they'd pity me

now as dusk encroaches
and she comes
looking for her looking-glass.
And it is me.

Yes it is me
she poaches her old face in.
I am bloated with her waters.
I am barren with her blood.
Another hour
and she will addle me

till I begin
to think like her.
As when I've grown
round and obscene with child,
or when I moan
for him between the sheets,
then I begin to know
that I am bright and original
and that my light's my own.

41

Degas's Laundresses

You rise, you dawn
roll-sleeved Aphrodites,
out of a camisole brine,
a linen pit of stitches,
silking the fitted sheets
away from you like waves.

You seam dreams in the folds
of wash from which freshes
the whiff and reach of fields
where it bleached and stiffened.
Your chat's sabbatical:
brides, wedding outfits,

a pleasure of leisured women
are sweated into the folds,
the neat heaps of linen.
Now the drag of the clasp.
Your wrists basket your waist.
You round to the square weight.

Wait. There. Behind you.
A man. There behind you.
Whatever you do don't turn.
Why is he watching you?
Whatever you do don't turn.
Whatever you do don't turn

See he takes his ease,
staking his easel so,
slowly sharpening charcoal,
closing his eyes just so,
slowly smiling as if
so slowly he is

unbandaging his mind.
Surely a good laundress
would understand its twists
its white turns,
its blind designs:

it's your winding sheet.

Woman in Kitchen

Breakfast over, islanded by noise,
she watches the machines go fast and slow.
She stands among them as they shake the house.
They move. Their destination is specific.
She has nowhere definite to go.
She might be a pedestrian in traffic.

White surfaces retract. White
sideboards light the white of walls.
Cups wink white in their saucers.
The light of day bleaches as it falls
on cups and sideboards. She could use
the room to tap with if she lost her sight.

Machines jigsaw everything she knows.
And she is everywhere among their furor:
the tropic of the dryer tumbling clothes.
The round lunar window of the washer.
The kettle in the toaster is a kingfisher
diving for trout above the river's mirror.

The wash done, the kettle boiled, the sheets
spun and clean, the dryer stops dead.
The silence is a death. It starts to bury

the room in white spaces. She turns to spread
a cloth on the board and irons sheets
in a room white and quiet as a mortuary.

A Ballad of Beauty and Time

Plainly came the time
the eucalyptus tree
could not succour me,
nor the honey pot,
the sunshine vitamin.
Not even getting thin.
I had passed my prime.

43

Then, when bagged ash,
scalded quarts of water,
oil of the lime,
cinders for the skin
and honey all had failed,
I sorted out my money
and went to buy some time.

I knew the right address:
the occult house of shame
where all the women came
shopping for a mouth,
a new nose, an eyebrow,
and entered without knocking
and stood as I did now.

A shape with a knife
stooped away from me,
cutting something vague –
I couldn't really see –
it might have been a face.
I coughed once and said
'I want a lease of life'.

The room was full of masks:
lines of grins gaping,
a wall of skin stretching,
a chin he had re-worked,
a face he had re-made.
He slit and tucked and cut,
then straightened from his blade.

'A tuck, a hem' he said –
'I only seam the line.
I only mend the dress.
It wouldn't do for you:
your quarrel's with the weave.
The best I achieve
is just a stitch in time'.

I started out again.
I knew a studio
strewn with cold heels,
closed in marble shock.
I saw the sculptor there
chiselling a nose,
and button-holed his smock:

'It's all very well
when you have bronzed a woman –
pinioned her and finned
wings on either shoulder.
Anyone can see
she won't get any older.
What good is that to me?

'See the last of youth
slumming in my skin,
my sham pink mouth.
Here behold your critic –
the threat to your aesthetic.
I am the brute proof:
beauty is not truth.'

'Truth is in our lies'
he angrily replied.
'This woman, fledged in stone,
is the centre of all eyes.
Her own will stay blind.
We sharpen with our skills
the arts of compromise.

'And all I have cast
in crystal or in glass,
in lapis or in onyx,
comes from knowing when
to lift and stay my hand
above the honest flaw
and say "let it stand".'

The Woman Changes her Skin

How often
in this loneliness,
unlighted
but for the porcelain

brightening
of the bath,
have I done this.
Again and again this.

This time,
in the shadowy
and woody light
between the bath and blind,

between the day and night,
the same blue
eyeshadow,
rouge and blusher,

will mesh
with my fingers
to a weaving
pulse.

In a ringed
coiling,
a convulsion,
I will heave

to a sinuous
and final
shining off
of skin:

look at the hood
I have made
for my eyes,
my head

and how quickly
over my lips,
slicked and cold,
my tongue flickers.

"Daphne with her thighs in bark"

POUND

I have written this
so that
in the next myth
my sister
will be wiser.

Let her learn from me:
the opposite of passion
is not virtue
but routine.

Look at me.
I can be cooking,
making coffee,
scrubbing wood perhaps,
and back it comes:
the crystalline,
the otherwhere,
the wood

where I was
when he began the chase.
And how I ran from him!

Pan thighed,
satyr-faced he was.

The trees reached out to me,
I silvered
and I quivered.
I shook out
my foil of quick leaves

47

He snouted past.
What a fool I was!

I shall be here forever,
setting out the tea,
among the paunched copper
and the branching alloys,
the tin shine
of this kitchen
and the pine table.

Save face sister.
Fall. Stumble.
Rut with him.
His rough heat
will keep you warm.

You will be better off
than me
with your memories
down the garden
at the start of March,
unable to keep your eyes
off the chestnut tree –

just the way
it thrusts and hardens.

Woman Posing

AFTER THE PAINTING *MRS BADHAM* BY INGRES

She is a housekeeping, a spring cleaning.
A swept, tidied, emptied, kept woman.

Her rimmed hat, its unkempt streamers,
neaten to the seams of a collar,
frilled and pat as a dressing table,
it's pressed lace and ruching hardly able
to hide the solid column of her neck:
reckless fashion, masking common-sense!

She smirks uneasily at what she's shirking,
sitting on this chair in silly clothes,
posing in a truancy of frills.

There's no repose in her broad knees.
The shawl she wears just upholsters her.
She hands the open book like pantry keys.

The New Pastoral

How hard it is –
the start
of this
my artifice!

The first man
had flint to spark.
He had a wheel
to read his world.

I'm in the dark.

I am a lost,
last inhabitant –
displaced person
in a pastoral chaos.

All day
I listen to
the loud distress –
the switch, the tick
of new herds –
but I'm no shepherdess.

Can I unbruise
these sprouts,
or wash
this mud flesh
till it roots again?

Can I make whole
this lamb's knuckle,
butchered from
its last, crooked suckling?

And how the dunce eye
of the washer
steams and winks!

I could be happy here,
I could be
something more
than a refugee

were it not
for these sprouts uprooted,
for that lamb unsuckled,
for the greasy
bacon flitch,
for the non-stop tick
witching me
till I feel

there was a past,
there was a pastoral,

and these
chance sights –
what are they all
but amnesias
of a rite
I danced once on a frieze?

It's a Woman's World

Our way of life
has hardly changed
since a wheel first
whetted a knife.

Maybe flame
burns more greedily
and wheels are steadier,
but we're the same:

we milestone
our lives
with oversights,
living by the lights

of the loaf left
by the cash register,
the washing powder
paid for and wrapped,
the wash left wet:

like most historic peoples
we are defined
by what we forget

and what we never will be:
star-gazers,
fire-eaters.
It's our alibi
for all time:

as far as history goes
we were never
on the scene of the crime.

When the king's head
gored its basket,
grim harvest,
we were gristing bread

51

or getting the recipe
for a good soup.
It's still the same:

our windows
moth our children
to the flame
of hearth not history.

And still no page
scores the low music
of our outrage.

Appearances reassure:
that woman there,
craned to
the starry mystery,

is merely getting a breath
of evening air.
While this one here,
her mouth a burning plume –

she's no fire-eater,
just my frosty neighbour
coming home.

The Woman Turns Herself Into A Fish

Unpod
the bag,
the seed.
Slap
the flanks back.

Make finny,
scaled
and chill

the slack
and dimple
of the rump.

Pout
the mouth.
Brow the eyes.
And now,
and now,

eclipse
in these hips,
these loins,
the moon,
the blood flux.

It's done.
I turn.
I flab upward
blub-lipped,
hipless
and I am
sexless,
shed of ecstasy:

a pale
swimmer
sequin-skinned,
pearling eggs
screamlessly
in seaweed.

It's what
I set my heart on.
Yet
ruddering
and muscling
in the sunless tons
of new freedoms,

still
I feel
a chill pull,
a brightening,
a light, a light.

And how
in my loomy cold,
my greens,
still
she moons
in me.

The Muse Mother

My window pearls wet.
The bare rowan tree
berries rain.

I can see
from where I stand
a woman hunkering–
her busy hand
worrying a child's face,

working a nappy liner
over his sticky, loud
round of a mouth.

Her hand's a cloud
across his face,
making light and rain,
smiles and a frown,
a smile again.

She jockeys him to her hip,
pockets the nappy liner,
collars rain on her nape
and moves away,

but my mind stays fixed:

If I could only decline her –
lost noun
out of context,
stray figure of speech –
from this rainy street
again to her roots,
she might teach me
a new language:

to be a sibyl
able to sing the past
in pure syllables,
limning hymns sung
to belly wheat or a woman,

able to speak at last
my mother tongue.

Monotony

The stilled hub
and polar drab
of the suburb
closes in.

In the round
of the staircase,
my arms sheafing nappies,
I grow in and down

to an old spiral,
a well of questions,
an oracle:
will it tell me –

am I
at these altars,
warm shrines –
washing machines, dryers,

with their incense
of men and infants –
priestess
or sacrifice?

My late tasks
wait like children:
milk bottles,
the milkman's note.

Cold air
clouds the rinsed,
milky glass,
blowing clear

with a hint
of winter constellations:
will I find
my answer where

Virgo reaps?
Her arms sheafing
the hemisphere,
hour after frigid hour,

her virgin stars,
her maidenhead
married to force,
harry us

to wed our gleams
to brute routines:
solstices,
small families.

Domestic Interior

FOR KEVIN

The woman is as round
as the new ring
ambering her finger.
The mirror weds her.
She has long since been bedded.

There is
about it all
a quiet search for attention,
like the unexpected shine
of a despised utensil.

The oils,
the varnishes,
the cracked light,
the worm of permanence –
all of them supplied by Van Eyck

by whose edict she will stay
burnished, fertile
on her wedding day,
interred in her joy.
Love, turn.

The convex of your eye
that is so loving, bright
and constant yet shows
only this woman in her varnishes
who won't improve in the light.

But there's a way of life
that is its own witness:
put the kettle on, shut the blind.
Home is a sleeping child,
an open mind

and our effects,
shrugged and settled
in the sort of light
jugs and kettles
grow important by.

Night Feed

This is dawn.
Believe me
This is your season, little daughter.
The moment daisies open,
The hour mercurial rainwater
Makes a mirror for sparrows.
It's time we drowned our sorrows.

I tiptoe in.
I lift you up
Wriggling
In your rosy, zipped sleeper.
Yes, this is the hour
For the early bird and me
When finder is keeper.

I crook the bottle.
How you suckle!
This is the best I can be,
Housewife
To this nursery
Where you hold on,
Dear life.

A silt of milk
The last suck.
And now your eyes are open,
Birth-coloured and offended.
Earth wakes.
You go back to sleep.
The feed is ended.

Worms turn.
Stars go in.
Even the moon is losing face.
Poplars stilt for dawn
And we begin
The long fall from grace.
I tuck you in.

Before Spring

They're grown.
The seedlings
have leaves.
They'll be ready soon

to prick out
and harden off.
Then mulching them
in terracotta pots

and finding
sunny beds
once the frosts
are over.

Then it's over –
the pride,
however slight,
in giving life.

That hard-blowing
wind outside
has a sound
of spring.

It won't be long.
No, it won't be long.
There is a melancholy
in the undersong.

Sweet child
asleep in your cot,
little seed-head,
there is time yet.

Hymn

Four a.m.
December.
A lamb would perish
out there.

The cutlery glitter
of that sky
has nothing in it
I want to follow.

Here is the star
of my nativity:
the nursery lamp
in that suburb window,

behind which
is boiled glass, a bottle,
and a baby all
hissing like a kettle.

The light goes out.
The blackbird
takes up his part.
I wake by habit.
I know it all by heart:

these candles
and the altar
and the psaltery of dawn.

And in the dark
as we slept
the world
was made flesh.

Energies

This is my time:
the twilight closing in,
a hissing on the ring.
stove noises, kettle steam,
and children's kisses.

But the energy of flowers!
Their faces are so white,
my garden daisies,
they are so tight-fisted –
such economies of light!

In the dusk they have made hay:
in a banked radiance,
in an acreage of brightness,
they are misering the day,
while mine delays away

in chores left to do:
the soup, the bath, the fire.
Then bed-time.
Up the stairs.
And there, there

the buttery curls,
the light,
the bran fur of the teddy-bear.
The fist like a night-time daisy.
Damp and tight.

In the Garden

Let's go out now
before the morning
gets warm.
Get your bicycle,

your teddy bear –
the one that's penny-coloured
like your hair –
and come.

I want to show you
what
I don't exactly know.
We'll find out.

It's our turn
in this garden,
by this light,
among the snails

and daisies –
one so slow
and one so closed –
to learn.

I could show you things:
how the poplar root
is pushing through,
how your apple tree is doing,

how daisies
shut like traps.
But you're happy
as it is

and innocence
that until this
was just
an abstract water,

welling elsewhere
to refresh,
is risen here
my daughter:

before the dew,
before the bloom,
the snail was here
The whole morning is his loom

and this is truth,
this is brute grace
as only instinct knows
how to live it:

turn to me
your little face.
It shows a trace still,
an inkling of it.

Fruit on a Straight-sided Tray

When the painter takes the straight-sided tray
and arranges late melons with grapes and lemons,
the true subject is the space between them;

in which repose the pleasure of these ovals
is seen to be an assembly of possibilities.
A deliberate collection of cross purposes:

gross blues and purples, yellow and the shadow of bloom.
The room smells of metal polish. The afternoon sun
brings light but not heat. And no distraction from

the study of absences, the science of relationships
in which the abstraction is made actual. Such as
fruit on a straight-sided tray. A homely arrangement.

This is the geometry of the visible, physical
tryst between substances – you, me, us –
disguising for a while the equation that kills:

you are my child and your body is
the destiny of mine. And between us are
spaces, distances growing to infinities.

Endings

A child
shifts in a cot.
No matter what happens now,
I'll never fill one again.

Beneath me,
the thick, crystal whitenesses
of daisies
drinking in their waters.

Behind me,
asleep
in their silences,
my baby daughters.

It's a night
white things ember in:
jasmine and the shine–
flowering, opaline –
of the apple trees.

If I lean
I can see
what it is the branches end in:

The leaf.
The reach.
The blossom.
The abandon.

Lights

We sailed the long way home
on a coal-burning ship.
There were bracelets on our freighter
of porpoises and water.

When we came where icebergs
shelved the stars of The Bear,
I leaned over the stern.
I was an urban twelve.

This was the Arctic garden:
a hard, sharkless Eden,
porched by the north.
A snow-shrubbed orchard
of Aurora Borealis,
apple-green and rosy,
behind an ice wall.

I loved the python waves,
the sinuous, tailing blaze,
coiled in polar water,
shoaling towards the cold
region where the daughters
of myth sang for the sailors,
who lay with them and lie
lost in phosphor graves.

I lie half-awake.
The last star is up
and my book is shut.
A child sleeps beside me.
I am three times twelve.

No more the Aurora –
but if I lift the window
and lean I can see
now over my lawn,
its ice-cap of shadow,
a nursery light rising.
A midnight sun dawning.

And nothing has changed:
the day is the same,
its cold illusory rays:
the dusk's ambiguous gleam.
Doubt still sharks
the close suburban night.

And all the lights I love
leave me in the dark.

After a Childhood Away from Ireland

One summer
we slipped in at dawn,
on plum-coloured water
in the sloppy quiet.

The engines
of the ship stopped.
There was an eerie
drawing-near,

a noiseless coming head-on
of red roofs, walls,
dogs, barley stooks.
Then we were there.

Cobh.
Coming home.
I had heard of this:
the ground the emigrants

resistless, weeping,
laid their cheeks to,
put their lips to kiss.
Love is also memory.

I only stared.
What I had lost
was not land
but the habit of land:

whether of growing out of,
or settling back on,
or being
defined by.

I climb
to your nursery.
I stand listening
to the dissonances

of the summer's day ending.
I bend to kiss you.
Your cheeks
are brick pink.

On Renoir's "The Grape Pickers"

They seem to be what they are harvesting:

rumps, elbows, hips clustering
plumply in the sun; a fuss of shines
wining from the ovals of their elbows.

The brush plucks them from a tied vine.
Such roundness, such a round vintage
of circles, such a work of pure spheres!
Flesh and shadow mesh inside each other.

But not this one: this red-headed woman.
Her skirt's a wave gathered to the weather.
Her eyes are closed. Her hands are loosening.
Her ears are fisted in a dozed listening.
She dreams of stoves, raked leaves, plums.

When she wakes summer will be over.

A Ballad of Home

How we kissed
in our half-built house!
It was slightly timbered,
a bit bricked, on stilts

and we were newly married.
We drove out at dusk
and picked our way to safety
through flint and grit and brick.

Like water through a porthole,
the sky poured in.
We sat on one step
making estimations

and hugged until the watchman
called and cursed and swung
his waterproof torch
into our calculations.

Ten years on:
you wouldn't find now
an inch of spare ground.
Children in their cots,

books, a cat, plants
strain the walls' patience
and the last ounce of space.
And still every night

it all seems so sound.
But love why wouldn't it?
This house is built on our embrace
and there are worse foundations.

Patchwork

I have been thinking at random
on the universe,
or rather, how nothing in the universe
is random –

(there's nothing like presumption late at night.)

My sumptuous
trash bag of colours –
Laura Ashley cottons –
waits to be cut
and stitched and patched but

there's a mechanical feel
about the handle
of my second-hand sewing machine,
with its flowers,
and 'Singer' painted orange,
and its iron wheel.

My back is to the dark.
Somewhere out there
are stars and bits of stars,
and little bits of bits,
and swiftnesses and brightnesses and drift –
but is it craft or art?

I will be here
till midnight,
cross-legged in the dining room,
logging triangles and diamonds,
cutting and aligning,
finding greens in pinks
and burgundies in white
until I finish it.

There's no reason in it.

Only when it's laid
right across the floor –
sphere on sphere
and seam on seam
in a good light –
will it start to hit me:

these are not bits
they are pieces
and the pieces fit.

I Remember

I remember the way the big windows washed
out the room and the winter darks tinted
it and how, in the brute quiet and aftermath,
an eyebrow waited helplessly to be composed

from the palette with its scarabs of oil
colours gleaming through a dusk leaking from
the iron railings and the ruined evenings of
bombed-out, post-war London; how the easel was

mulberry wood and, porcupining in a jar,
the spines of my mother's portrait brushes
spiked from the dirty turpentine and the face
on the canvas was the scattered fractions

of the face which had come up the stairs
that morning and had taken up position in
the big drawing-room and had been still
and was now gone; and I remember, I remember

I was the interloper who knows both love and fear,
who comes near and draws back, who feels nothing
beyond the need to touch, to handle, to dismantle it,
the mystery; and how in the morning when I came down –

a nine-year-old in high, fawn socks –
the room had been shocked into a glacier
of cotton sheets thrown over the almond
and vanilla silk of the French Empire chairs.

Mise Eire

I won't go back to it –

my nation displaced
into old dactyls,
oaths made
by the animal tallows
of the candle –

land of the Gulf Stream,
the small farm,
the scalded memory,
the songs
that bandage up the history,
the words
that make a rhythm of the crime

where time is time past.
A palsy of regrets.
No. I won't go back.
My roots are brutal:

I am the woman –
a sloven's mix
of silk at the wrists,
a sort of dove-strut
in the precincts of the garrison –

who practises
the quick frictions,
the rictus of delight
and gets cambric for it,
rice-coloured silks.

I am the woman
in the gansy-coat
on board the "Mary Belle",
in the huddling cold,

holding her half-dead baby to her
as the wind shifts East
and North over the dirty
water of the wharf

mingling the immigrant
guttural with the vowels
of homesickness who neither
knows nor cares that

a new language
is a kind of scar
and heals after a while
into a passable imitation
of what went before.

Self-Portrait on a Summer Evening

Jean-Baptiste Chardin
is painting a woman
in the last summer light.

All summer long
he has been slighting her
in botched blues, tints,
half-tones, rinsed neutrals.

What you are watching
is light unlearning itself,
an infinite unfrocking of the prism.

Before your eyes
the ordinary life
is being glazed over:
pigments of the bibelot,
the cabochon, the water-opal
pearl to the intimate
simple colours of
her ankle-length summer skirt.

Truth makes shift:
the triptych shrinks
to the cabinet picture.

Can't you feel it?
Aren't you chilled by it?
The way the late afternoon
is reduced to detail –

the sky that odd shade of apron –

opaque, scumbled –
the lazulis of the horizon becoming
optical greys
before your eyes
before your eyes
in my ankle-length
summer skirt

crossing between
the garden and the house,
under the whitebeam trees,
keeping an eye on
the length of the grass,
the height of the hedge,
the distance of the children

I am Chardin's woman

edged in reflected light,
hardened by
the need to be ordinary.

The Oral Tradition

I was standing there
at the end of a reading
or a workshop or whatever,
watching people heading
out into the weather,

only half-wondering
what becomes of words,
the brisk herbs of language,
the fragrances we think we sing,
if anything.

We were left behind
in a firelit room
in which the colour scheme
crouched well down –
golds, a sort of dun

a distressed ochre –
and the sole richness was
in the suggestion of a texture
like the low flax gleam
that comes off polished leather.

Two women
were standing in shadow,
one with her back turned.
Their talk was a gesture,
an outstretched hand.

They talked to each other
and words like "summer"
"birth" "great-grandmother"
kept pleading with me,
urging me to follow.

"She could feel it coming" –
one of them was saying –
"all of the way there,
across the fields at evening
and no one there, God help her

and she had on a skirt
of cross-woven linen
and the little one
kept pulling at it.
It was nearly night..."

(Wood hissed and split
in the open grate,
broke apart in sparks,
a windfall of light
in the room's darkness)

"...when she lay down
and gave birth to him
in an open meadow.
What a child that was
to be born without a blemish!"

It had started raining,
the windows dripping, misted.
One moment I was standing
not seeing out,
only half-listening

staring at the night; the next
without warning
I was caught by it:
the bruised summer light,
the musical sub-text

of mauve eaves on lilac
and the laburnum past
and shadow where the lime
tree dropped its bracts
in frills of contrast

where she lay down
in vetch and linen
and lifted up her son
to the archive
they would shelter in:

the oral song
avid as superstition,
layered like an amber in
the wreck of language
and the remnants of a nation.

I was getting out
my coat, buttoning it,
shrugging up the collar.
It was bitter outside,
a real winter's night

and I had distances
ahead of me: iron miles
in trains, iron rails
repeating instances
and reasons; the wheels

singing innuendoes, hints,
outlines underneath
the surface, a sense
suddenly of truth,
its resonance.

Fever

is what remained or what they thought
remained after the ague and the sweats
were over and the shock of wild flowers
at the bedside had been taken away;

is what they tried to shake out of
the crush and dimple of cotton,
the shy dust of a bridal skirt;
is what they beat, lashed, hurt like

flesh as if it were a lack of virtue
in a young girl sobbing her heart out
in a small town for having been seen
kissing by the river; is what they burned

alive in their own back gardens
as if it were a witch and not the full-
length winter gaberdine and breathed again
when the fires went out in charred dew.

My grandmother died in a fever ward,
younger than I am and far from
the sweet chills of a Louth spring –
its sprigged light and its wild flowers –

with five orphan daughters to her name.
Names, shadows, visitations, hints
and a half-sense of half-lives remain.
And nothing else, nothing more unless

I re-construct the soaked-through midnights;
vigils; the histories I never learned
to predict the lyric of; and re-construct
risk; as if silence could become rage,

as if what we lost is a contagion
that breaks out in what cannot be
shaken out from words or beaten out
from meaning and survives to weaken

what is given, what is certain
and burns away everything but this
exact moment of delirium when
someone cries out someone's name.

The Unlived Life

"Listen to me" I said to my neighbour,
"how do you make a hexagon-shape template?"

So we talked about end papers,
cropped circles, block piece-work
while the children shouted and
the texture of synthetics as compared
with the touch of strong cloth
and how they both washed.

"You start out with jest so much caliker" –
Eliza Calvert Hall of Kentucky said –
"that's the predestination
but when it comes to cuttin' out
the quilt, why, you're free to choose".

Suddenly I could see us
calicoed, overawed, dressed in cotton
at the railroad crossing, watching
the flange-wheeled, steam-driven, iron omen
of another life passing, passing
wondering for a moment what it was
we were missing as we turned for home

to choose
in the shiver of silk and dimity
the unlived life, its symmetry
explored on a hoop with a crewel needle
under the silence of the oil light;

to formalize the terrors of routine
in the algebras of a marriage quilt
on alternate mornings when you knew
that all you owned was what you shared.

It was bed-time for the big children
and long past it for the little ones
as we turned to go
and the height of the season went by us;

tendrils, leaps, gnarls of blossom,
asteroids and day-stars of our small world,
the sweet-pea ascending the trellis
the clematis descended
while day backed into night
and separate darks blended the shadows,
singling a star out of thin air

as we went in.

Lace

Bent over
the open notebook –

light fades out
making the trees stand out
and my room
at the back
of the house, dark.

In the dusk
I am still
looking for it –
the language that is

lace:

a baroque obligation
at the wrist
of a prince
in a petty court.
Look, just look
at the way he shakes out

the thriftless phrases,
the crystal rhetoric
of bobbined knots
and bosses:
a vagrant drift
of emphasis
to wave away an argument
or frame the hand
he kisses;
which, for all that, is still

what someone
in the corner
of a room,
in the dusk,
bent over
as the light was fading

lost their sight for.

The Bottle Garden

I decanted them – feather mosses, fan-shaped plants,
asymmetric greys in the begonia –
into this globe which shows up how the fern shares
the invertebrate lace of the sea-horse.

The sun is in the bottle garden,
submarine, out of its element
when I come down on a spring morning;
my sweet, greenish, inland underwater.

And in my late thirties, past the middle way,
I can say how did I get here?
I hardly know the way back, still less forward.
Still, if you look for them, there are signs:

Earth stars, rock spleenwort, creeping fig
and English ivy all furled and herded
into the green and cellar wet
of the bottle; well, here they are

here I am a gangling schoolgirl
in the convent library, the April evening outside,
reading the *Aeneid* as the room darkens
to the underworld of the Sixth book –

the Styx, the damned, the pity and
the improvised poetic of imprisoned meanings;
only half aware of the open weave of harbour lights
and my school blouse riding up at the sleeves.

Suburban Woman: a Detail

I

The chimneys have been swept.
The gardens have their winter cut.
The shrubs are prinked, the hedges gelded.

The last dark shows up the headlights
of the cars coming down the Dublin mountains.

Our children used to think they were stars.

II

This is not the season
when the goddess rose
out of seed, out of wheat,
out of thawed water
and went, distracted and astray,
to find her daughter.

Winter will be soon:
Dun pools of rain;
ruddy, addled distances;
winter pinks, tinges and
a first-thing smell of turf
when I take the milk in.

III

Setting out for a neighbour's house
in a denim skirt,

a blouse blended in
by the last light,

I am definite
to start with
but the light is lessening,
the hedge losing its detail,
the path its edge.

Look at me, says the tree.
I was a woman once like you,
full-skirted, human.

Suddenly I am not certain
of the way I came
of the way I will return,
only that something
which may be nothing
more than darkness has begun
softening the definitions
of my body, leaving

the fears and all the terrors
of the flesh shifting the airs
and forms of the autumn quiet

crying "remember us".

The Women

This is the hour I love: the in-between,
neither here-nor-there hour of evening.
The air is tea-coloured in the garden.
The briar rose is spilled crepe-de-Chine.

This is the time I do my work best,
going up the stairs in two minds,
in two worlds, carrying cloth or glass,
leaving something behind, bringing
something with me I should have left behind.

The hour of change, of metamorphosis,
of shape-shifting instabilities.
My time of sixth sense and second sight
when in the words I choose, the lines I write,
they rise like visions and appear to me:

women of work, of leisure, of the night,
in stove-coloured silks, in lace, in nothing,
with crewel needles, with books, with wide open legs

who fled the hot breath of the god pursuing,
who ran from the split hoof and the thick lips
and fell and grieved and healed into myth,

into me in the evening at my desk
testing the water with a sweet quartet,
the physical force of a dissonance –

the fission of music into syllabic heat –
and getting sick of it and standing up
and going downstairs in the last brightness

into a landscape without emphasis,
light, linear, precisely planned,
a hemisphere of tiered, aired cotton,

a hot terrain of linen from the iron,
folded in and over, stacked high,
neatened flat, stoving heat and white.

83

Nocturne

After a friend has gone I like the feel of it:
The house at night. Everyone asleep.
The way it draws in like atmosphere or evening.

One-o-clock. A floral teapot and a raisin scone.
A tray waits to be taken down.
The landing light is off. The clock strikes. The cat

comes into his own, mysterious on the stairs,
a black ambivalence around the legs of button-back
chairs, an insinuation to be set beside

the red spoon and the salt-glazed cup,
the saucer with the thick spill of tea
which scalds off easily under the tap. Time

is a tick, a purr, a drop. The spider
on the dining room window has fallen asleep
among complexities as I will once

the doors are bolted and the keys tested
and the switch turned up of the kitchen light
which made outside in the back garden

an electric room – a domestication
of closed daisies, an architecture
instant and improbable.

On Holiday

Ballyvaughan.
Peat and salt.
How the wind bawls
across these mountains
scalds the orchids
of the Burren.

They used to leave milk
out once on these windowsills
to ward away
the child-stealing spirits.

The sheets are damp.
We sleep between the blankets.
The light cotton of the curtains
lets the light in.

You wake first thing
and in your five-year-size
striped nightie you are
everywhere trying everything:
the springs on the bed,
the hinges on the window.

You know your a's and b's
but there's a limit now
to what you'll believe.

When dark comes I leave
a superstitious feast
of wheat biscuits, apples,
orange juice out for you
and wake to find it eaten.

The Wild Spray

It came to me one afternoon in summer –
a gift of long-stemmed flowers in a wet
contemporary sheath of newspapers
which pieced off easily at the sink.

I put them in an ironstone jug
near the window; now years later
I know the names for the flowers
they were but not the shape they made:

The true rose beside the mountain rose,
the muslin finery of asparagus fern,

85

rosemary, forsythia; something about it was
confined and free in the days that followed

which were the brute, final days of summer –
a consistency of milk about the heat haze,
midges freighting the clear space between
the privet and the hedge, the nights chilling

quickly into stars, the morning breaking late
and on the low table the wild spray
lasted for days, a sweet persuasion,
a random guess becoming a definition.

I have remembered it in a certain way –
displaced yellows and the fluencies
of colours in a jug making a statememt of
the unfurnished grace of white surfaces

the way I remember us when we first came here
and had no curtains; the lights on the mountain
that winter were sharp, distant promises
like crocuses through the snowfall of darkness.

We stood together at an upstairs window
enchanted by the patterns in the haphazard,
watching the streetlamp making rain into
a planet of tears near the whitebeam trees.

The Journey

FOR ELIZABETH RYLE

Immediately cries were heard. These were the loud wailing of infant souls weep-
ing at the very entrance-way; never had they had their share of life's sweetness
for the dark day had stolen them from their mother's breasts and plunged them
to a death before their time.   – Virgil, *The Aeneid*, Book VI

And then the dark fell and "there has never"
I said "been a poem to an antibiotic:
never a word to compare with the odes on
the flower of the raw sloe for fever

"or the devious Africa-seeking tern
or the protein treasures of the sea-bed.
Depend on it, somewhere a poet is wasting
his sweet uncluttered metres on the obvious

"emblem instead of the real thing.
Instead of sulpha we shall have hyssop dipped
in the wild blood of the unblemished lamb,
so every day the language gets less

"for the task and we are less with the language."
I finished speaking and the anger faded
and dark fell and the book beside me
lay open at the page Aphrodite

comforts Sappho in her love's duress.
The poplars shifted their music in the garden,
a child startled in a dream,
my room was a mess –

the usual hardcovers, half-finished cups,
clothes piled up on an old chair –
and I was listening out but in my head was
a loosening and sweetening heaviness,

not sleep, but nearly sleep, not dreaming really
but as ready to believe and still
unfevered, calm and unsurprised
when she came and stood beside me

and I would have known her anywhere
and I would have gone with her anywhere
and she came wordlessly
and without a word I went with her

down down down without so much as
ever touching down but always, always
with a sense of mulch beneath us,
the way of stairs winding down to a river

and as we went on the light went on
failing and I looked sideways to be certain

it was she, misshapen, musical –
Sappho – the scholiast's nightingale

and down we went, again down
until we came to a sudden rest
beside a river in what seemed to be
an oppressive suburb of the dawn.

My eyes got slowly used to the bad light.
At first I saw shadows, only shadows.
Then I could make out women and children
and, in the way they were, the grace of love.

"Cholera, typhus, croup, diptheria"
she said, "in those days they racketed
in every backstreet and alley of old Europe.
Behold the children of the plague".

Then to my horror I could see to each
nipple some had clipped a limpet shape –
suckling darknesses – while others had their arms
weighed down, making terrible pietàs.

She took my sleeve and said to me, "be careful.
Do not define these women by their work:
not as washerwomen trussed in dust and sweating,
muscling water into linen by the river's edge

"nor as court ladies brailled in silk
on wool and woven with an ivory unicorn
and hung, nor as laundresses tossing cotton,
brisking daylight with lavender and gossip.

"But these are women who went out like you
when dusk became a dark sweet with leaves,
recovering the day, stooping, picking up
teddy bears and rag dolls and tricycles and buckets –

"love's archaeology – and they too like you
stood boot deep in flowers once in summer
or saw winter come in with a single magpie
in a caul of haws, a solo harlequin".

88

I stood fixed. I could not reach or speak to them.
Between us was the melancholy river,
the dream water, the narcotic crossing
and they had passed over it, its cold persuasions.

I whispered, "let me be
let me at least be their witness," but she said
"what you have seen is beyond speech,
beyond song, only not beyond love;

"remember it, you will remember it"
and I heard her say but she was fading fast
as we emerged under the stars of heaven,
"there are not many of us; you are dear

"and stand beside me as my own daughter.
I have brought you here so you will know forever
the silences in which are our beginnings,
in which we have an origin like water,"

and the wind shifted and the window clasp
opened, banged and I woke up to find
my poetry books stacked higgledy piggledy,
my skirt spread out where I had laid it –

nothing was changed; nothing was more clear
but it was wet and the year was late.
The rain was grief in arrears; my children
slept the last dark out safely and I wept.

Envoi

It is Easter in the suburb. Clematis
shrubs the eaves and trellises with pastel.
The evenings lengthen and before the rain
the Dublin mountains become visible.

My muse must be better than those of men
who made theirs in the image of their myth.
The work is half-finished and I have nothing
but the crudest measures to complete it with.

Under the street-lamps the dustbins brighten.
The winter flowering jasmine casts a shadow
outside my window in my neighbour's garden.
These are the things that my muse must know.

She must come to me. Let her come
to be among the donnée, the given.
I need her to remain with me until
the day is over and the song is proven.

Surely she comes, surely she comes to me –
no lizard skin, no paps, no podded womb
about her but a brightening and
the consequences of an April tomb.

What I have done I have done alone.
What I have seen is unverified.
I have the truth and I need the faith.
It is time I put my hand in her side.

If she will not bless the ordinary,
if she will not sanctify the common,
then here I am and here I stay and then am I
the most miserable of women.

Listen. This is the Noise of Myth

This is the story of a man and woman
under a willow and beside a weir
near a river in a wooded clearing.
They are fugitives. Intimates of myth.

Fictions of my purpose. I suppose
I shouldn't say that yet or at least
before I break their hearts or save their lives
I ought to tell their story and I will.

When they went first it was winter; cold,
cold through the Midlands and as far West
as they could go. They knew they had to go –
through Meath, Westmeath, Longford,

their lives unravelling like the hours of light –
and then there were lambs under the snow
and it was January, aconite and jasmine
and the hazel yellowing and puce berries on the ivy.

They could not eat where they had cooked,
nor sleep where they had eaten
nor at dawn rest where they had slept.
They shunned the densities

of trees with one trunk and of caves
with one dark and the dangerous embrace
of islands with a single landing place.
And all the time it was cold, cold:

the fields still gardened by their ice,
the trees stitched with snow overnight,
the ditches full; frost toughening lichen,
darning lace into rock crevices.

And then the woods flooded and buds
blunted from the chestnut and the foxglove
put its big leaves out and chaffinches
chinked and flirted in the branches of the ash.

And here we are where we started from –
under a willow and beside a weir
near a river in a wooded clearing.
The woman and the man have come to rest.

Look how light is coming through the ash.
The weir sluices kingfisher blues.
The woman and the willow tree lean forward, forward.
Something is near; something is about to happen;

something more than Spring
and less than history. Will we see

hungers eased after months of hiding?
Is there a touch of heat in that light?

If they stay here soon it will be summer; things
returning, sunlight fingering minnowy deeps,
seedy greens, reeds, electing lights
and edges from the river. Consider

legend, self-deception, sin, the sum
of human purpose and its end; remember
how our poetry depends on distance,
aspect: gravity will bend starlight.

Forgive me if I set the truth to rights.
Bear with me if I put an end to this:
She never turned to him; she never leaned
under the sallow-willow over to him.

They never made love; not there; not here;
not anywhere; there was no winter journey;
no aconite, no birdsong and no jasmine,
no woodland and no river and no weir.

Listen. This is the noise of myth. It makes
the same sound as shadow. Can you hear it?
Daylight greys in the preceptories.
Her head begins to shine

pivoting the planets of a harsh nativity.
They were never mine. This is mine.
This sequence of evicted possibilities.
Displaced facts. Tricks of light. Reflections.

Invention. Legend. Myth. What you will.
The shifts and fluencies are infinite.
The moving parts are marvellous. Consider
how the bereavements of the definite

are easily lifted from our heroine.
She may or she may not. She was or wasn't
by the water at his side as dark
waited above the Western countryside.

O consolations of the craft.
How we put
the old poultices on the old sores,
the same mirrors to the old magic. Look.

The scene returns. The willow sees itself
drowning in the weir and the woman
gives the kiss of myth her human heat.
Reflections. Reflections. He becomes her lover.

The old romances make no bones about it.
The long and short of it. The end and the beginning
The glories and the ornaments are muted.
And when the story ends the song is over.

An Irish Childhood In England: 1951

The bickering of vowels on the buses,
the clicking thumbs and the big hips of
the navy-skirted ticket collectors with
their crooked seams brought it home to me:
Exile. Ration-book pudding.
Bowls of dripping and the fixed smile
of the school pianist playing "Iolanthe",
"Land of Hope and Glory" and "John Peel".

I didn't know what to hold, to keep.
At night, filled with some malaise
of love for what I'd never known I had,
I fell asleep and let the moment pass.
The passing moment has become a night
of clipped shadows, freshly painted houses,
the garden eddying in dark and heat,
my children half-awake, half-asleep.

Airless, humid dark. Leaf-noise.
The stirrings of a garden before rain.
A hint of storm behind the risen moon.
We are what we have chosen. Did I choose to? –

in a strange city, in another country,
on nights in a North-facing bedroom,
waiting for the sleep that never did
restore me as I'd hoped to what I'd lost –

let the world I knew become the space
between the words that I had by heart
and all the other speech that always was
becoming the language of the country that
I came to in nineteen-fifty-one:
barely-gelled, a freckled six-year-old,
overdressed and sick on the plane
when all of England to an Irish child

was nothing more than what you'd lost and how:
was the teacher in the London convent who
when I produced "I amn't" in the classroom
turned and said – "you're not in Ireland now".

Fond Memory

It was a school where all the children wore darned worsted;
where they cried – or almost all – when the Reverend Mother
announced at lunch-time that the King had died

peacefully in his sleep. I dressed in wool as well,
ate rationed food, played English games and learned
how wise the Magna Carta was, how hard the Hanoverians

had tried, the measure and complexity of verse,
the hum and score of the whole orchestra.
At three-o-clock I caught two buses home

where sometimes in the late afternoon
at a piano pushed into a corner of the playroom
my father would sit down and play the slow

lilts of Tom Moore while I stood there trying
not to weep at the cigarette smoke stinging up
from between his fingers and – as much as I could think –

I thought this is my country, was, will be again,
this upward-straining song made to be
our safe inventory of pain. And I was wrong.

The Glass King

Isabella of Bavaria married Charles VI of France in 1385.
In later years his madness took the form of believing he was
made from glass.

When he is ready he is raised and carried
among his vapourish plants; the palms and ferns flex;
they almost bend; you'd almost think they were going to kiss him;
and so they might; but she will not, his wife,

no she can't kiss his lips in case he splinters
into a million Bourbons, mad pieces.
What can she do with him – her daft prince?
His nightmares are the Regency of France.

Yes, she's been through it all, his Bavaroise,
blub-hipped and docile, urgent to be needed –
from churning to milk fever, from tongue-tied princess
to the queen of a mulish king – and now this.

They were each other's fantasy in youth.
No splintering at all about that mouth
when they were flesh and muscle, woman and man,
fire and kindling. See that silk divan?

Enough said. Now the times themselves
are his asylum: these are the Middle Ages, sweet
and savage era of the saving grace; indulgences
are two a penny; under the stonesmith's hand

stone turns into lace. I need his hand now.
Outside my window October soaks the stone;
you can hear it; you'd almost think
the brick was drinking it; the rowan drips

and history waits. Let it wait. I want
no elsewheres: the clover-smelling, stove-warm
air of Autumn catches cold; the year turns;
the leaves fall; the poem hesitates:

if we could see ourselves, not as we do –
in mirrors, self-deceptions, self-regardings –
but as we ought to be and as we have been:
poets, lute-stringers, makyres and abettors

of our necessary art, soothsayers of the ailment
and disease of our times, sweet singers,
truth tellers, intercessors for self-knowledge –
what would we think of these fin-de-siècle

half-hearted penitents we have become
at the sick-bed of the century: hand-wringing
elegists with an ill-concealed greed
for the inheritance?
                    My prince, demented

in a crystal past, a lost France, I elect you emblem
and ancestor of our lyric: it fits you like a glove –
doesn't it? – the part; untouchable, outlandish,
esoteric, inarticulate and out of reach

of human love: studied every day by your wife,
an ordinary honest woman out of place
in all this, wanting nothing more than the man
she married, all her sorrows in her stolid face.